JAMES

balanced

A 21-DAY DEVOTIONAL
TO HELP YOU LIVE WITH BOTH GRACE *AND* TRUTH

Assembled and Produced for James Merritt by
Breakfast for Seven
breakfastforseven.com

Printed in the United States of America.

Contents

Finding Divine Balance

I was standing in front of my chemistry teacher, my face flushed with shame. She had just caught me red-handed, frantically flipping through my textbook hidden under my desk during an exam. "See me after class," she said as she snatched my paper away. When my classmates filed out, I stood before her—the only C I'd ever received hanging in the balance.

Jesus was 100% grace and 100% truth all the time. He never shared grace at the expense of truth, and He never spoke truth at the expense of grace.

It wasn't until twenty years later that I finally found the courage to write that teacher a letter of apology. Her response stunned me: "I'm so glad to see the reality of the grace of Jesus in your life. Isn't it wonderful to be freed by the truth?"

In that simple reply, my teacher captured what it means to live a balanced life in Christ, embracing grace and truth together.

Our culture tells us that balance means never judging, never taking a firm stance, and accepting everything as equally valid. We're constantly encouraged to be tolerant, open-minded, and affirming of all choices. The message is clear: "It's wrong to say something is wrong."

But true biblical balance looks nothing like that. When the disciple John described Jesus, he made a profound observation: Jesus was "... *full of grace and truth*" (John 1:14, NIV)—not 50% grace and 50% truth or grace on Monday and truth on Tuesday. Jesus was 100% grace and 100% truth all the time. He never shared grace at the expense of truth, and He never spoke truth at the expense of grace.

This perfect balance is what made Jesus so magnetic to the sinners He encountered and so threatening to the religious leaders of His day. When a woman caught in adultery was thrown at His feet, He didn't condemn her, but He also didn't excuse her sin: "'... Then neither do I condemn you,' Jesus declared. 'Go now and leave your life of sin'" (John 8:11, NIV). This is balanced Christianity.

Over the next 21 days, we'll explore what it means to live in this divine tension between grace and truth. We'll see how Jesus modeled this balance perfectly and consider what it looks like in our own lives and churches.

Some of us naturally lean toward truth—quick to confront wrongs but sometimes slow to show compassion. Others of us lean toward grace— quick to accept but sometimes reluctant to speak hard truths. My prayer is that by the end of these 21 days, we'll all be more balanced in our approach to God, others, and ourselves.

To help define this balance in your life, we've included three daily exercises.

The "Reflection Question" section invites you to consider various areas where grace and truth apply to your life as you draw nearer to God.

The "Balanced Living" section offers practical steps, such as writing biblical truths or identifying past thought processes, to help you integrate greater balance into your life.

The "My Balanced Day" section provides a space to journal your thoughts and prayers as you record your progress along the journey.

Because when you're full of Jesus, you'll be full of both grace and truth.

Let's begin.

Dr. James Merritt

"For the law was given through Moses; grace and truth came through Jesus Christ."

JOHN 1:17 (NIV)

Balance from the Beginning

The Old Testament introduces us to 613 commandments that tune us into the reality that a holy God requires righteousness. Yet beneath these laws beats the heart of grace. Today's verse says the law was *"given"* through Moses, meaning God graciously offered His laws to instruct His people about how to remain in relationship with Him.

Remember the story in Genesis when God regretted creating the world and was ready to destroy it all? Even there, God's grace surfaced: *"But Noah found favor in the eyes of the LORD"* (Genesis 6:8, NIV).

The word *favor* there in the original Hebrew language literally means "grace." God, in His grace, chose not to destroy everything and everyone. But much of the Old Testament emphasizes God's laws and the failure and inability of His people to follow them. That's why John points out in today's verse: *"For the law was given through Moses...."* But he doesn't stop there. When Jesus comes along, the light of grace shines so brightly that truth gets a new partner. Notice that John not only highlights grace and truth when he describes Jesus—he purposefully orders grace first.

When Jesus arrives on the scene, the light of grace bursts through like the morning sun. In Him, you see the fullness of what the Old

Testament could only foreshadow. You see the fullness of grace *and* truth. The question is: When you look at Jesus, what do you see first?

Reflection Question

. . . .

Where do you see evidence of God's grace in your life before you even knew Him? How does recognizing grace in all seasons of your life change your perspective?

Balanced Living

. . . .

Make a list of three moments of "Noah's favor" in your life—times when God's grace saved you from destruction you might have deserved.

Prayer

....

Heavenly Father, thank You that Your grace has always been part of Your character, from Noah's day to now. Open my eyes to see the grace You've shown me throughout my life. Help me to be a vessel of Your grace to everyone I meet today. In Jesus' Name, Amen.

My Balanced Day

"'For God so loved the world that he gave his one and only Son, that whoever believes in him shall not perish but have eternal life.'"

JOHN 3:16 (NIV)

Grace and Truth:
Our Spiritual DNA

Have you ever stopped to consider the miracle of DNA? This microscopic blueprint carries instructions for every cell in your body, with two strands wrapped around each other in perfect symmetry.

I believe God encoded this same principle in our spiritual lives. Grace and truth are our spiritual DNA—the essential building blocks of a Christ-centered life. Like physical DNA's double helix, grace and truth wrap around each other in beautiful harmony, running in seemingly opposite directions yet balancing each other perfectly.

This isn't just a nice theological concept—it's demonstrated at the cross. Grace and truth are joined at the hip at the cross: Grace says, "No matter how sinful you are, your sin can be forgiven," while truth says, "The reason your sin can be forgiven is because Jesus died for your sin."

One without the other creates a spiritual mutation. But grace and truth together replicate into life, healing, and strength. Then you will offer forgiveness that transforms. You'll set standards based on God's Word, and encourage others in the grace that helps to meet those standards.

Let your life testify to this balance. As others encounter you, may they feel the same way the adulterous woman did with Jesus—completely accepted yet lovingly challenged to grow.

This is the miracle of spiritual DNA working as designed, creating in you the likeness of Christ Himself.

Reflection Question

How might your perspective on eternity change if you truly believed both grace and truth would be fully revealed when you meet Jesus face-to-face?

Balanced Living

Spend time today meditating on John 3:16, noting how it perfectly balances grace (*"God so loved the world"*) with truth (*"whoever believes in Him shall not perish"*). ◑

Prayer

....

Heavenly Father, thank You for encoding both grace and truth into the very structure of creation and redemption. I praise You for the cross, where grace and truth meet perfectly. Help me to live today with healthy spiritual DNA, embracing both Your love and Your unchanging standards. In Jesus' Name, Amen.

My Balanced Day

"But God demonstrates his own love for us in this: While we were still sinners, Christ died for us."

ROMANS 5:8 (NIV)

day
3

Two Wings to Fly

Have you ever seen a bird try to fly with just one wing? It's impossible. No matter how vigorously that single wing might flap, the bird remains grounded, spinning in frustrated circles.

Similarly, many Christians today are grounded in their spiritual growth because they're trying to fly with just one wing. The Gospel flies with two wings: grace and truth. When we're full of ourselves, we become either full of truth but empty of grace, or full of grace but empty of truth. The more we're filled with Jesus, the more we're filled with both.

The "truth-only" believer flaps furiously but never gets off the ground. They know Scripture perfectly and can win theological arguments, but their relationships are strained, and their joy is minimal. Meanwhile, the "grace-only" believer spins in circles of good intentions, never gaining the altitude of spiritual maturity. They excel at acceptance but struggle with accountability.

But when both wings work together? That's when you soar! With grace and truth combined, you can persevere through trials with peace, navigate difficult relationships with wisdom, and overcome temptation not through willpower alone but through knowing what's right and receiving power to do it.

Today, ask yourself: *Which wing am I missing?* Are you striving, trying to live the Christian life in your own strength? That's truth without grace. Are you stuck in the same patterns, excusing sin rather than overcoming it? That's grace without truth. Receive both from Jesus to soar above your circumstances.

Reflection Question

Think of a challenging situation you faced recently where you might have prioritized one "wing" over the other. Did you focus on being right (truth) without showing compassion, or did you avoid necessary confrontation (grace without accountability)? How might balancing both wings have led to spiritual growth for everyone involved?

Balanced Living

For the next three days, before each significant conversation, pause and ask yourself: *Am I approaching this with both wings ready to fly?* When truth-oriented, add acceptance. When grace-oriented, speak necessary truth with love.

Prayer

Heavenly Father, Your love for me is perfect. You demonstrated both grace and truth when You sent Jesus to die for me while I was still in my sin. I confess that I often try to fly with just one wing, either judging without mercy or accepting without transformation. Help me recognize which wing I need to strengthen in each relationship and situation I face. In Jesus' Name, Amen.

My Balanced Day

"The Word became flesh and made his dwelling among us. We have seen his glory, the glory of the one and only Son, who came from the Father, full of grace and truth."

JOHN 1:14 (NIV)

All Truth, No Grace

Have you ever felt like you weren't good enough for God? I once counseled a woman who wrote down her "spiritual failures" in a journal, convinced God was keeping the same tally. Her faith was all truth without grace—a crushing weight that left her spiritually paralyzed.

Remember, John described Jesus as "... *full of grace and truth*" (John 1:14, NIV)—not one or the

other but both in perfect harmony. Jesus embod-
ied 100% truth and 100% grace simultaneously.
And He perfectly illustrated that balance on
the cross when He died so that we can always
be forgiven.

This isn't just theological theory; it makes all
the difference to the way you approach God.
Unlike the woman with her failure journal, you
don't have to grovel or plead for acceptance.
We can come boldly, not because we're perfect
or have something to offer, but because Jesus
perfectly balanced what we couldn't: He satisfied
God's righteous demands AND offers abundant
mercy. The cross doesn't lower God's standards;
it fulfills them completely, freeing you to receive
grace without guilt and live in truth without
any condemnation.

Maybe you struggle to accept God's grace,
keeping Him at arm's length as you expect judgment rather than mercy. This reveals hidden pride
—believing your sin is somehow beyond God's

forgiveness. The beautiful reality is that God's grace is greater than your greatest failure.

When you finally stand before Him, you'll see grace and truth perfectly unified in the nail-scarred hands of Jesus—a powerful reminder that you are completely known and completely loved.

Reflection Question

In what areas of your life do you struggle to accept God's grace, believing instead that you must earn His approval?

Balanced Living

Today, identify one area where you've been relying on your performance rather than God's grace, and intentionally thank Him for His unconditional acceptance of you.

Prayer

···

Heavenly Father, thank You for perfectly balancing grace and truth in Jesus. I confess that I often try to earn Your approval rather than receiving Your free gift of grace. Thank You for the cross, where Your love and holiness meet perfectly. Help me to live in the freedom of Your grace while respecting the boundaries of Your truth. In Jesus' Name, Amen.

My Balanced Day

"Grace and truth have met together; justice and peace have kissed each other."

PSALM 85:11 (CJB)

day
5

Prime Truths

Scripture contains what I like to call "prime truths." You might remember prime numbers from math in school, and prime truths are somewhat similar. They are foundational principles that cannot be divided, distorted, or dismissed. They are truths we must consistently return to, regardless of cultural trends or personal preferences.

Grace and truth are prime truths. They cannot be divided or distorted without ending up with the wrong answer. Constantly seeking to incorporate both is a non-negotiable, whether it's in your relationship with God or with others or in how you approach issues in the marketplace.

Like me, you probably drift in one of two ways: an imbalance toward truth (embracing standards at the expense of compassion) or an imbalance toward grace (valuing freedom over accountability). Both distortions leave you spiritually unstable. Like a building's foundation, these prime truths keep your faith structurally sound.

They also appear in everyday life. As a parent, you can lovingly correct your child while affirming their value. As a friend, you can speak a hard truth and then remain supportive through consequences. In marriage, you might hold one another accountable while forgiving when you both fall short.

When practiced together, these prime truths create environments where real connection and transformation can happen.

Reflection Question

....

Which of these "prime truths" have you been neglecting or reinterpreting to fit your comfort level?

Balanced Living

....

Take time today to write down three non-negotiable biblical truths that you need to recommit to, regardless of what feels comfortable or convenient.

Prayer

....

Heavenly Father, thank You for the unshakable foundation of Your truth. Sometimes I try to bend Your truth to fit my preferences rather than submitting to Your Word. Thank You for being faithful and unchanging, even when I am inconsistent. Help me to stand firmly on Your prime truths, especially when they are uncomfortable. In Jesus' Name, Amen.

My Balanced Day

"Just then a woman of the village, the town harlot, having learned that Jesus was a guest in the home of the Pharisee, came with a bottle of very expensive perfume and stood at his feet, weeping, raining tears on his feet. Letting down her hair, she dried his feet, kissed them, and anointed them with the perfume."

LUKE 7:37-38 (MSG)

Grace First

Have you ever felt too broken to approach God? This woman, a known prostitute, should have been terrified to enter the house of a Pharisee— one of the religious elite of Jesus' day. By every cultural standard, she was unwelcome, unworthy, and unwanted. Yet something compelled her to brave the stares and whispers.

She had encountered Jesus before. In His eyes, she saw not condemnation but compassion. When He spoke, she heard grace. When He walked by, she felt acceptance she'd never known. While everyone else saw her sin, Jesus saw her heart.

Her extravagant response—letting down her hair (a scandalously intimate act), washing His feet with tears, and pouring costly perfume—reveals an important truth: She didn't clean up her life first and then come to Jesus. She came to Jesus exactly as she was.

Have you ever thought that sin disqualifies you from God's grace? Here's a liberating secret: Sin doesn't disqualify you from grace; sin is the only thing that qualifies you for God's grace.

You don't give up your sin and then receive God's grace. You receive God's grace first, and then you are empowered to overcome your sin.

Reflection Question

. . . .

What areas of your life have you been trying to "fix" before bringing them to God?

Balanced Living

. . . .

Identify one thing you've avoided talking with God about—perhaps due to feelings of shame. Intentionally bring it to Him in prayer, receiving His grace first.

Prayer

....

Heavenly Father, thank You for offering grace first. I confess that I've often tried to clean myself up before coming to You. Thank You for loving me in my brokenness. Help me to receive Your grace fully today, knowing it's the starting point of transformation. In Jesus' Name, Amen.

My Balanced Day

"'Sanctify them by the truth;

your word is truth.'"

JOHN 17:17 (NIV)

The Courage of Truth

I was standing in my office when I received an email from a visitor to our church. He was upset because I had called a certain behavior "sin." He said: "I will not attend a church that won't accept my friends because their views are different from the guy at the pulpit." What troubled me most wasn't his disagreement but his assumption that truth and acceptance cannot coexist.

In our culture today, many want a Jesus made in their own image—"sugar and spice and everything nice." This Jesus never confronts, never challenges, and certainly never calls anything "sin." But that's not the Jesus of Scripture.

The apostle John describes Jesus as being *"... full of grace and truth."* Note that both qualities were present in full measure.

The famous theologian H. Richard Niebuhr describes how many adopt a false faith of "a God without wrath, [bringing] men without sin into a kingdom without judgment through the ministrations of a Christ without a cross."[1] But this counterfeit Christianity offers no real hope because it lacks the power of truth.

Aligning with truth means you see yourself, others, and the world as God does, not as you prefer. It also means living in the light—exposing every part of your heart to God—not just the presentable parts.

Instead of compartmentalizing your life, talk to Him not only about your church attendance but also your private browsing history. Confess your impatience and share any financial pressures or temptations. Pray about your career and your sexual temptations. Hiding from truth builds walls in your relationship with God.

Without truth, you have no need for grace. Without grace, truth would crush you. Through Jesus, you can receive both.

Reflection Question

In what area of your life are you most reluctant to invite God's truth? Why do you think that is?

Balanced Living

....

Choose one area of your life you typically keep "off limits" from God and intentionally invite His truth there today through honest prayer.

Prayer

....

Heavenly Father, thank You for being both loving and holy. I confess that I often prefer comfort over conviction. Thank You for sending Jesus, Who perfectly balanced grace and truth. Help me to see myself as You see me, without hiding or pretending. In Jesus' Name, Amen.

My Balanced Day

_____

_____

_____

_____

_____

_____

_____

_____

_____

_____

_____

_____

_____

_____

_____

_____

_____

_____

_____

_____

"'Two people owed money to a certain moneylender. One owed him five hundred denarii, and the other fifty. Neither of them had the money to pay him back, so he forgave the debts of both. Now which of them will love him more?'"

LUKE 7:41–42 (NIV)

Returning to Grace

Have you ever felt the weight of a debt you couldn't possibly repay? Maybe it was financial, or maybe it was a relational debt—someone forgave you when you deserved nothing but their rejection. That's precisely the scenario Jesus presented to Simon the Pharisee in today's passage.

In this parable, Jesus reveals a profound truth: Whether our debt is fifty denarii or five hundred, we're all spiritually bankrupt. One person's sin may appear ten times worse than another's, but the reality is that none of us can settle our account with God. The religious leader and the person without a home stand equally in need of grace.

This is where many of us misunderstand the Christian life. We imagine grace as the entrance exam to faith, and we graduate to more "advanced" spiritual disciplines. But grace isn't just the starting point—it's the atmosphere you breathe every day. You never outgrow your need for grace; you only grow deeper in your appreciation of it.

When you truly understand grace, you will see yourself differently—not as superior to anyone but as equally dependent on God's mercy. You'll see others differently too—not as "worse sinners" but as fellow recipients of the same unmerited favor. And most importantly, you see Jesus as He truly is—the essence of grace that you desperately need today just as much as you did the day you first believed.

The paradox of following Jesus is this: The longer you walk with Him, the more aware you become of your need for grace—and the more amazed you are that it never runs out.

Reflection Question

In what areas of your spiritual life have you been trying to "graduate" from grace and rely on your own goodness or effort instead?

Balanced Living

Listen to the song "Amazing Grace." Afterward, select one stanza and turn it into a prayer of thanksgiving. Resist the habit of asking God for something and simply appreciate His indescribable grace.

Prayer

....

Heavenly Father, thank You for Your amazing grace. I often forget how desperately I need Your grace and sometimes think I've moved beyond it. Thank You for the cross that reminds me that Your grace is not just where I begin but where I live every moment. Help me to see myself, others, and You through the lens of amazing grace. In Jesus' Name, Amen.

My Balanced Day

"'God is spirit, and his worshipers must worship in the Spirit and in truth.'"

JOHN 4:24 (NIV)

Spirit and Truth

She sat by the well at noon, deliberately avoiding the other women who came in the cooler hours. Jesus asked her for water, breaking every social norm. When he offered her *"living water"* (John 4), she was intrigued but confused. As their conversation deepened, Jesus gently exposed her broken past—she had five husbands and was now living with

someone else. Rather than condemning her,
He revealed a profound truth about worship.

True worship isn't about location—not on the
mountain or in Jerusalem—but about connection
with God in both Spirit and truth. We need both
elements in perfect balance.

Worship in Spirit without truth can become
emotional. Worship in truth without the Spirit
can become cold, lacking that warmth of connection and relationship. But when balanced, you
can acknowledge your sin honestly while experiencing God's grace fully.

When the Samaritan woman encountered this
balance in Jesus, she left her water jar behind
and hurried to tell everyone she knew about
Him. The living water she had found was a relationship grounded in being completely exposed
and loved at the same time.

Come before God with all of your heart and
mind. Acknowledge your sin truthfully, and then

worship Him completely from a place of humility and freedom.

Reflection Question

....

Where do you tend to lean—toward emotional spirituality or intellectual truth? How might finding balance deepen your worship?

Balanced Living

....

Today, spend time in honest confession before God, and then transition into heartfelt worship, experiencing the freedom that comes from this divine balance.

Prayer

· ·

Heavenly Father, thank You for being a God Who desires both Spirit and truth. I confess that I often favor one over the other in my approach to You. Thank You for meeting me at my point of need, just as You met the woman at the well. Help me to worship You with my whole being—honestly acknowledging my sin and joyfully embracing Your grace. In Jesus' Name, Amen.

My Balanced Day

"For the law was given through Moses; grace and truth came through Jesus Christ. No one has ever seen God, but the one and only Son, who is himself God and is in closest relationship with the Father, has made him known."

JOHN 1:17–18 (NIV)

Acceptance Before Correction

Ever wonder why people in the Bible who were nothing like Jesus seemed drawn to Him? Tax collectors, prostitutes, and social outcasts flocked to this holy man when they typically avoided religious leaders. The answer lies in today's verse.

While Moses brought the truth of the Law, a clear standard that showed people how to live,

Jesus brought that and more—the perfect balance of grace and truth.

Notice again the order: Grace first, then truth. Jesus didn't compromise standards, but He led with compassion. This explains why those who seemed farthest from God felt comfortable in His presence. They encountered acceptance before correction.

Think about your own interactions. Do people experience your judgment before your love? Does your truth lack the sweetener of grace? When you're tempted to point fingers at others' failings, remind yourself how Jesus has treated you—with open arms before challenges to change. His approach isn't "Clean up, then come in," but "Come in, and I'll help you clean up."

Accept God's love first. Then you'll naturally show more compassion before correcting others, letting mercy overcome judgment in your life.

Reflection Question

When people interact with you, what do they experience first—judgment and correction? Or love and grace?

Balanced Living

Today, try leading with grace in every conversation. Watch how it transforms your relationships and reflects the heart of Jesus—full of grace and truth.

Prayer

....

Heavenly Father, thank You for Your character, full of grace and truth. I don't often strike that balance—being full of grace and truth. But Lord, You offer me grace and give me Your promise and power. Thank You for teaching me how to respond rather than react and how to offer compassion instead of judgment. Let me reflect Your heart in word and deed. In Jesus' Name, Amen.

My Balanced Day

"Brothers and sisters, if someone is caught in a sin, you who live by the Spirit should restore that person gently. But watch yourselves, or you also may be tempted."

GALATIANS 6:1 (NIV)

Truth That Heals, Not Hurts

"Tolerance applies only to persons, but never to principles," wrote Bishop Fulton Sheen. "Intolerance applies only to principles, but never to persons."[2] These profound words from 1936 remain relevant today as we navigate relationships where truth and grace must coexist.

When someone you care about is making harmful choices, the world often presents you two extreme responses: harsh confrontation or complete acceptance. Neither reflects the biblical balance. A relationship without truth becomes a hollow connection built on pretense.

Jesus modeled balance perfectly. He never sacrificed truth for acceptance, yet His approach to sinners was so gracious they flocked to Him while religious leaders kept their distance.

In your relationships, remember that loving someone means wanting what's best for them, even when it requires difficult conversations. As Paul instructs, you should restore gently, aware of your own vulnerability to temptation. This approach—truth infused with grace—creates deep and authentic relationships.

Real love speaks truthfully—but always with the goal of restoration, not punishment.

Reflection Question

Think about a relationship where you've avoided speaking truth out of fear or discomfort. How might that relationship actually deepen through gentle, loving honesty?

Balanced Living

When you need to address a difficult truth with someone this week, prepare your heart first by reflecting on how God has shown you grace in your own struggles.

Prayer

....

Heavenly Father, thank You for loving me enough to speak truth into my life. When I avoid difficult conversations out of fear, remind me that real love requires both grace and truth. And help me live it out! May I restore others gently, always remembering my own need for Your mercy. In Jesus' Name, Amen.

My Balanced Day

"When the Pharisee who had invited him saw this, he said to himself, 'If this man were a prophet, he would know who is touching him and what kind of woman she is—that she is a sinner.'"

LUKE 7:39 (NIV)

day
12

Seeing Through Jesus' Eyes

Have you ever misjudged someone based on appearances? In Luke 7, we find Jesus at a dinner party and a woman known for her sinful lifestyle enters uninvited. She begins washing Jesus' feet with her tears. The host, a Pharisee named Simon, is horrified. In his mind, her label—"sinner"—is all that matters. But Jesus sees beyond the label to her heart.

The Greek word for *sinner* used here was commonly used for those considered morally corrupt by religious standards. Yet Jesus, Who indeed knew exactly who she was, welcomed her anyway. While Simon focused on her past, Jesus focused on her present faith and future redemption.

How often do we assign permanent labels to people based on their worst moments or choices? Jesus challenges us to see people not through the lens of their past or choices, but as sons and daughters created in His image—capable of transformation.

When you look at others, do you see their potential through the eyes of grace, or do you only see their past through the lens of judgment? Try to catch yourself when you mentally label another person—whether at home, at work, or while you're driving along the highway. Instead, ask God to help you see them as Jesus would— with eyes of grace and potential for renewal.

Reflection Question

....

Think about someone you've labeled or categorized in your mind. How might Jesus see this person differently than you do?

Balanced Living

....

Today, when you interact with someone you've previously judged, intentionally look for qualities in them that reflect God's image.

Prayer

....

Heavenly Father, thank You for seeing beyond my labels and loving me despite knowing everything about me. I confess that I often judge others by appearances or past mistakes. Thank You for demonstrating how to balance truth with grace. Help me to see others as You see them—with potential, purpose, and immeasurable worth. In Jesus' Name, Amen.

My Balanced Day

"As she stood behind him at his feet weeping, she began to wet his feet with her tears. Then she wiped them with her hair, kissed them and poured perfume on them."

LUKE 7:38 (NIV)

Extravagant Grace

Have you ever been deeply hurt by someone's judgment and later have to encounter them face-to-face? The woman in Luke 7 knew this feeling intimately. Labeled a "sinner" by society, she boldly entered a Pharisee's home—a place where she'd been deemed unworthy—and approached Jesus with extraordinary courage and vulnerability.

Instead of bitterness toward those who had condemned her, she brought expensive perfume and tears of gratitude. Her response wasn't revenge but reverence and adoration. While Simon offered Jesus the bare minimum of hospitality, she gave extravagantly.

Notice Jesus' reaction. He didn't just accept her worship; He elevated it. He used her actions to teach everyone present about true love and forgiveness. Her extravagance became a powerful testimony that challenged their self-righteousness.

When we respond to judgment with grace rather than resentment, we mirror Jesus' character. This doesn't mean ignoring harm done to us but rather choosing not to let bitterness define who we are or how we respond. Extravagant grace breaks cycles of hurt and creates space for healing that judgment never could.

Take a moment to think about someone who has judged or hurt you. What would it look like to respond with grace rather than the retaliation they might expect?

Reflection Question

. . . .

Think about a time when someone judged or mistreated you. How might responding with unexpected grace have changed both of you?

Balanced Living

. . . .

Identify one person who has hurt you and take one small step toward them with grace—perhaps a kind word, a prayer for their well-being, or even just letting go of resentment in your heart.

Prayer

....

Heavenly Father, thank You for the extravagant grace You've shown me— despite knowing everything about me. And thank You for this woman's powerful example of gratitude and courage. Help me respond to judgment with grace like You did in this moment. Create new possibilities of healing through me, I pray. In Jesus' Name, Amen.

My Balanced Day

"'...You did not give me any water for my feet, but she wet my feet with her tears and wiped them with her hair. You did not give me a kiss, but this woman, from the time I entered, has not stopped kissing my feet.'"

LUKE 7:44–45 (NIV)

The Cost of Judgment

When Jesus attended Simon's dinner party, the Pharisee extended an invitation but withheld true hospitality. He neglected the customary foot washing, the welcoming kiss, and the anointing oil—basic courtesies of the culture. Jesus had been treated rudely and had every right to get angry, turn around, and walk out the door.

In Simon's home, judgment replaced welcome. In verse 39, the Pharisee silently criticized both Jesus (*"'If this man were a prophet...'"*) and the woman (*"'... he would know ... what kind of woman she is...'"*). It's like Simon kept a mental scorecard that prevented him from seeing either person clearly.

Notice the contrast Jesus highlights: While Simon withheld basic courtesy, the woman gave extravagantly. While he judged silently, she loved openly. While he maintained his distance, she drew near with vulnerability. Jesus' gentle rebuke revealed how Simon's judgment had created barriers not just between himself and this woman but between himself and Jesus.

When we lead with judgment rather than grace, we often miss the divine moments unfolding before us. Like Simon, who failed to recognize the Messiah at his own table despite having memorized prophecies about Him, our critical spirits can blind us to God's presence and work.

Truth without grace builds walls. Grace-filled truth builds bridges. Which are you constructing in your relationships today?

Reflection Question

How has judgment—either yours toward others or someone else's toward you—created barriers in an important relationship?

Balanced Living

Identify one relationship where you've been more like Simon than like Jesus. Take a small step today to extend grace where you've previously offered only judgment.

Prayer

....

Heavenly Father, thank You for your perfect balance of truth and grace. I confess that I often judge others harshly while excusing myself. Thank You for showing me in Your Word how judgment damages relationships while grace restores them. Help me to see both my own need for grace and opportunities to extend it to others today. In Jesus' Name, Amen.

My Balanced Day

"'Then you will know the truth,

and the truth will set you free.'"

JOHN 8:32 (NIV)

Handling the Truth

In one of my all-time favorite movie scenes, Jack Nicholson's character in *A Few Good Men* thunders at the young, prosecuting attorney played by Tom Cruise: "You can't handle the truth!" That line resonates because we live in a culture that often cannot, or simply does not want to, handle the truth.

Jesus addressed this tendency of ours when speaking to His disciples. He didn't say, "You will know *a* truth," but rather, *"You will know* **the** *truth."* This distinction is crucial in understanding Jesus' message.

There are two types of truth. There is earthly truth that is accurate but not life-changing, and then there is eternal truth that is powerful and can take a person from darkness to light and from death to life.

Our culture increasingly treats truth as relative and personal, but Jesus presented truth as absolute and universal. When we embrace subjective truth, we become enslaved to shifting opinions. But when we anchor ourselves to God's unchanging truth, we experience genuine freedom—freedom from deception, from fear, and, ultimately, from sin itself.

The question isn't whether you can handle the truth—it's whether you'll let the truth handle you.

Reflection Question

What cultural messages or personal preferences have you embraced that might contradict the clear truth of Scripture?

Balanced Living

Identify one area where you've been compromising biblical truth and then take a concrete step toward aligning your beliefs with God's Word.

Prayer

....

Heavenly Father, thank You for being the source of all truth. I confess that I sometimes prefer comfortable half-truths over Your challenging whole truth. Thank You for Your Word that lights my path and sets me free. Help me to love Your truth, and even when it makes me uncomfortable, help me embrace it so You can make me holy. In Jesus' Name, Amen.

My Balanced Day

_____

_____

_____

_____

_____

_____

_____

_____

_____

_____

_____

_____

_____

_____

_____

_____

"Therefore confess your sins to each other and pray for each other so that you may be healed. The prayer of a righteous person is powerful and effective."

JAMES 5:16 (NIV)

Caught Red-Handed

As a young child, I stole a soldier's hat belonging to the son of my babysitter, Mrs. Gunter. I took it home and hid it under my bed, causing me a week of restless nights and growing guilt. The following week, I confessed. Mrs. Gunter was truthful and gracious. "I knew you took the hat, and I knew you would bring it back. I forgive you."

When confronting wrongdoing—whether personal failings or societal issues—we face a choice. Do we lead with harsh judgment or ignore truth altogether? Jesus shows a better way.

In today's verse, James instructs believers to pray for governmental authorities—the same officials who often persecuted Christians. This response isn't passive acceptance of injustice but recognition that transformation begins with grace. Approaching broken systems with compassion creates space for truth to be heard.

When I walked back into Mrs. Gunter's kitchen and placed it on the table, I wasn't sure how she would respond. Her combined honesty and compassion were more effective in my development than any punishment—I learned the safety of grace and truth in the midst of sin.

When facing brokenness, experiencing injustice or dealing with your own sin, begin with grace, and don't withhold truth. Both are essential for genuine transformation.

Reflection Question

....

When you encounter corruption, injustice, or moral issues in society, do you tend to lead with harsh judgment or avoid speaking truth altogether? How might Jesus' balanced approach change your response?

Balanced Living

....

Before speaking out about a controversial issue today, first pray for those involved, asking God to give you both compassion for the people and clarity about truth.

Prayer

··

Heavenly Father, thank You for Your perfect balance of grace and truth. Help me to approach difficult issues with the same heart You have—one that offers grace without compromising truth. Give me wisdom to know when to speak and how to speak in ways that reflect Your character. In Jesus' Name, Amen.

My Balanced Day

"When they kept on questioning him, he straightened up and said to them, 'Let any one of you who is without sin be the first to throw a stone at her.'"

JOHN 8:7 (NIV)

The Finger-Pointing Test

They thought they had Him cornered. Religious leaders dragged a woman caught in adultery before Jesus, creating the perfect trap. If He condemned her, His compassionate reputation would crumble. If He pardoned her, they could accuse Him of dismissing the law. Instead, Jesus bent down and wrote in the dust.

Then He declared these profound words: *"'Let any one of you who is without sin be the first to throw a stone at her.'"* With these words, Jesus issued a fundamental truth: None of us is without sin.

In our digital age, we've become experts at accusation. Social media has given us platforms to publicly condemn others—to point fingers at political opponents, fallen celebrities, or anyone whose behavior we disapprove of. We build cases against others while conveniently forgetting our own shortcomings.

But Jesus invites us to a different posture. His response wasn't to minimize the woman's sin but to widen the conversation to include everyone's brokenness. Except for God's grace, we could easily stand in the other person's place—exposed and condemned.

Remember that adage? If you point a finger at someone, three fingers point back at you. This doesn't mean you should never address wrongdoing, but Jesus shows you how to approach it with humility—always aware of your own need for mercy.

Reflection Question

....

When was the last time you were quick to judge someone else's failure? How might remembering your own need for grace change your approach to addressing others' wrongdoing?

Balanced Living

....

The next time you're tempted to criticize someone, pause and reflect on when you've needed grace for similar weaknesses. Let that memory inform how you speak truth.

Prayer

....

Heavenly Father, thank You for Your mercy toward me despite my sins. Forgive me for the times when I have excused myself for judging others harshly. Thank You for showing me that I am not qualified to condemn. Guide me to balance addressing sin with extending the same grace You've shown me. In Jesus' Name, Amen.

My Balanced Day

"Hearing that, they walked away, one after another, beginning with the oldest. The woman was left alone. Jesus stood up and spoke to her. 'Woman, where are they? Does no one condemn you?' 'No one, Master.' 'Neither do I,' said Jesus. 'Go on your way. From now on, don't sin.'"

JOHN 8:9–11 (MSG)

The Unfinished Story

Picture the scene: A woman caught in adultery stands before Jesus. Her accusers have fled, leaving just the two of them—the guilty and the guiltless. She braces for condemnation from the One Who wrote the law she broke. Instead, she feels the gentle breeze of grace: *"'Neither do I condemn you...'"* (John 8:11, NIV).

But Jesus doesn't stop there. He adds words our culture often omits: "'... *Go now and leave your life of sin*'" (v. 11, NIV). Most people today would end the story with unconditional acceptance. Jesus offers something better—both grace and truth.

The religious leaders offered truth without grace, ready to stone her. Our culture often offers grace without truth, affirming everything without calling for change. Jesus perfectly balances both—extending compassion without compromising on what is right.

When Jesus called her "woman," He used a term of respect—the same word He used for His mother. She hadn't heard this word in a long time. His hands held no stones but offered something more powerful: forgiveness that acknowledged sin while providing a path forward.

The beauty isn't just that Jesus didn't condemn her but that He loved her enough not to leave her in her sin. True love doesn't say, "You're fine as you are." It says, "You're too precious to stay as you are."

Jesus invites you to resist ending the story too soon in your own relationships and communities. And He offers the perfect template: indescribable love paired with life-transforming truth.

Reflection Question

What cultural challenges tempt you to offer grace without truth or truth without grace? How might adopting Jesus' complete approach alter your perspective?

Balanced Living

....

Pray about one frustrating situation—
whether in your family, in your community,
or in the world—where you've been
reluctant to speak truth. Ask God for
courage to talk about it with genuine love
rather than judgment.

Prayer

....

*Heavenly Father, thank You for not
leaving me in my sin but loving me
enough to transform me. I confess that
I often emphasize either grace or truth at
the expense of the other. Thank You for
showing me, through Jesus, what perfect
balance looks like. When I look at the
people in my life and issues in the world,
help me see an unfinished story. In Jesus'
Name, Amen.*

My Balanced Day

"Now the Lord is the Spirit; and where the Spirit of the Lord is, there is liberty."

2 CORINTHIANS 3:17 (NKJV)

Staying in the Saddle

Martin Luther once said that the Devil doesn't care which side of the horse we fall off of, as long as we don't stay in the saddle. I've thought about that quote often while watching Christians tip too far one way or another. Some tumble into the ditch of liberalism while others topple into the ditch of legalism. The Christian journey requires keeping both feet firmly in the stirrups—one foot in grace, the other in truth.

Most of us naturally lean toward one side. A little honesty with yourself will reveal whether you're a "truther" or a "gracer." Truthers prioritize standards and doctrinal purity. Gracers emphasize acceptance and forgiveness. Your answer reveals where you need to become more like Jesus.

If you're a truther, you may be right in your stance but still lose influence. Your correct doctrine delivered without love becomes just a "...*resounding gong...*" (1 Corinthians 13:1, NIV). You may need to extend some grace.

If you're a gracer, you excel at making people feel loved, but someone might be suffering because you've given them all grace and no truth. They might need loving words of guidance. Remember, real love "...*rejoices with the truth*" (1 Corinthians 13:6, NIV).

Here's a simple formula: Grace without truth equals liberalism—quick to excuse, slow to confront. Truth without grace sends you to the opposite side of the spectrum—quick to judge, slow to forgive. But grace and truth together equal liberty—the freedom Christ died to give us.

Today, check your balance in the saddle. Which stirrup are you neglecting? Your aim isn't to be right—it's to be like Jesus.

Reflection Question

Are you a "truther" or a "gracer"? What concrete step can you take today to develop the side you tend to neglect?

Balanced Living

In today's polarized culture, identify an issue where you've leaned too heavily toward either rigid judgment or blanket acceptance. Consider how you might approach that topic with both biblical truth and Christlike compassion when it comes up in conversation or on social media.

Prayer

Heavenly Father, thank You for showing me that spiritual balance comes from being full of Jesus. Thank You for loving me enough to meet me where I am while challenging me to become more like You. Help me stay firmly in the saddle with one foot in the stirrup of truth and the other in the stirrup of grace. In Jesus' Name, Amen.

My Balanced Day

"He has shown you, O mortal, what is good. And what does the LORD require of you? To act justly and to love mercy and to walk humbly with your God."

MICAH 6:8 (NIV)

day
20

For Goodness' Sake

When's the last time you saw true goodness in action?

In June 1783, after defeating the most powerful armed forces in the world, General George Washington sent a leaflet to the colonies with a closing prayer that quoted Micah 6:8. He knew that for America to be a "happy Nation," its people needed to "do Justice, to love mercy and to demean ourselves, with that Charity, humility ..."[3] that characterized Jesus.

Washington understood this reality: You can't talk about goodness without talking about grace and truth. The Lord tells us clearly that goodness is doing and loving the right things.

- First, it's acting in truth and justice—treating people equitably regardless of their status.
- Second, it's loving mercy and grace—not giving people what they deserve when they wrong us.
- Third, it's walking humbly with God—surrendering to His leadership rather than being led by our own self-importance.

You demonstrate true goodness as you live with grace and truth. And how do you do that? Through consistent, quiet surrender to God's leading.

As you go through your day, consider God's call to truth and justice as you interact with others. Do you give them what they're due (whether protection or correction)? Do you show mercy even when it's undeserved? Do you walk with God in humble submission?

Remember, goodness isn't what you do for God. Real goodness is what God does through you.

Reflection Question

Think about a recent situation where you had to balance justice and mercy. Did you lean more toward enforcing rules (truth) or showing compassion (grace)? What might have changed if you had integrated both more fully?

Balanced Living

Think about one relationship where you need more balance. If you've been emphasizing rules and consequences, find a way to express genuine care and acceptance. If you've been avoiding hard conversations out of kindness, consider how speaking truth might actually be the most loving action.

Prayer

Heavenly Father, make me an instrument of Your goodness today. Help me to act justly in all my dealings, to love mercy even when it's difficult, and to walk humbly with You in everything I do. May others see Your character reflected in my actions. In Jesus' Name, Amen.

My Balanced Day

"What this adds up to, then, is this: no more lies, no more pretense. Tell your neighbor the truth. In Christ's body we're all connected to each other, after all. When you lie to others, you end up lying to yourself."

EPHESIANS 4:25 (MSG)

Truth in Love

I heard a story once about a time when Albert Einstein was giving a physics exam. After the exam was handed out, a student exclaimed, "Dr. Einstein, the questions on this year's exam are the same questions from last year's exam!" To which Albert Einstein replied, "That's okay. The answers this year are different!"

While Einstein's response gets a laugh, it reminds us that although science evolves as we discover new information, God's truth remains constant. What is truly truth never changes. Truth that is absolute never becomes obsolete. It may be out of fashion, out of favor, or out of friends, but it is never out of date. Truth is always true no matter what century it is.

In your family, workplace, and community, God has given you a responsibility to speak up and address issues that go against His will. This doesn't mean you are the self-appointed morality police but rather a humble truth-teller. As Paul explains in Ephesians, speaking truth isn't optional—it's essential because we are all connected.

When a company unconsciously promotes racial bias, when a team member under-mines others, when ethical corners are cut for profit—these moments demand that you engage truthfully. You aren't called to judge the person but to address the action. You can speak from the powerful recognition that truth offered in love brings freedom.

Jesus modeled a perfect pattern: accepting others without approving of sinful behavior. In your life, this balanced approach offers hope that only comes from Christ—the hope and promise of genuine transformation.

Reflection Question

··

Where in your workplace or community have you hesitated to speak truth about an issue that contradicts God's values? What holds you back?

Balanced Living

Identify one situation where you need to speak truth. Before addressing it, spend time in prayer asking God for words that offer both grace and truth.

Prayer

Heavenly Father, thank You for not leaving me in my sin but calling me to something better. And thank You for showing me, through Christ, how to balance grace with truth. Help me to address wrong actions without condemning the people behind them. Give me courage to speak truth in love, especially when it's uncomfortable. In Jesus' Name, Amen.

My Balanced Day

"Out of his fullness we have all received grace in place of grace already given. For the law was given through Moses; grace and truth came through Jesus Christ."

JOHN 1:16–17 (NIV)

Conclusion

Finding Your Balance

As we conclude our journey through these devotions, my prayer is that you've discovered your own tendencies—whether you naturally lean toward being a "gracer" or a "truther"—and have begun taking steps toward divine balance. Remember that true balance isn't compromise; it's fullness. It's not being half-grace and half-truth but 100% grace and 100% truth.

I also pray that this devotional is a new beginning for you. The world around you desperately needs men and women who live in both grace and truth. And may you discover, as I have, that the closer you draw to Jesus, the more naturally this balance will flow from your life.

Because when you're full of Jesus, you'll be full of both grace and truth.

Dr. James Merritt